Post-Traumatic Church Disorder:
A Prescription for Healing from Church Hurt

Post-Traumatic Church Disorder:
A Prescription for Healing from Church Hurt
by Mickey Stonier PhD

© Copyright 2023 by Mickey & Marié Stonier. All rights reserved.

Scripture quotations marked (ESV) are from the ESV* bible (The Holy Bible, English Standard Version*), copyright © 2001 Crossway, a publishing ministry of Good News Publishers. Used by permission. All rights reserved.

Scripture quotations marked (NIV) are from THE HOLY BIBLE, NEW INTERNATIONAL VERSION*, NIV*. Copyright © 1973, 1978, 1984 by Biblica US, Inc.*. Used by permission.

Scripture quotations marked (NKJV) are taken from the New King James Version. Copyright © 1982 by Thomas Nelson, Inc. All rights reserved. Used by permission.

Without limiting the rights under copyright reserved above, no part of this publication—whether in printed or eBook format, or any other published derivation—may be reproduced, stored in or introduced into a retrieval system, or transmitted, in any form or by any means (electronic, mechanical, photocopying, recording, or otherwise), without the prior written permission of the author.

The scanning, uploading, and distribution of this book via the Internet or via any other means without the permission of the author is illegal and punishable by law. Please purchase only authorized electronic editions and do not participate in or encourage electronic piracy of copyrightable materials.

Paperback: ISBN# 979-8-86642-824-3

To the many wounded Kingdom warriors who continue to fight the good fight of faith through forgiveness, grace, hope, and love.

Table of Contents

Preface

Chapter 1: Ministry Behind the Veil

Chapter 2: Two Deadly Questions

Chapter 3: With-ness Empowers Witness

Chapter 4: Embitterment Disorder

Chapter 5: Freedom in Forgiveness

Final Thoughts

Reflection Questions

Preface

This is a book I intended to write over ten years ago. As I embarked on that journey, I took a right turn at *GODISNOWHERE*. It was in my heart to write about the hardships and wounds of ministry that I had experienced over decades of serving people who had been hurt by people in the church. However, as I began authoring that story, my thoughts couldn't shake the expanse of pain that was happening well outside of the domain of the church—hence, a number of years ago I sought to marinate in "Where is God in the midst of your pain?" By the way, if you haven't read my book, *GODISNOWHERE,* to date it's the best book I've written (and yes, thus far it's the only book I've written.) OK, I did co-author *Get Out of Control: Finding Freedom in Letting Go.* However, I was mostly an appendage with that book as my wife gets the full credit for writing it.

Now, nearly a decade later, I'm back to my original book's intent. Why now you may ask? Was it a move of God's Spirit? Is it a theme that is urgent for today? No, actually my wife, Marié, told me I needed to write it. Happy life, wise wife. And once again, as I committed to this endeavor, I have been reminded about the agonizing lives of the many amazing people with whom I have served in ministry. I actually don't believe that Post-Traumatic Church Disorder (PTCD) is a new malady. And it isn't technically a clinically diagnosed disorder, yet many people have been infected with this ailment, hence the need for an antidote. Researchers have actually correlated religious trauma as a contributor to PTSD. Cases of church hurt have produced symptoms of intrusive memories, hyperarousal, hypervigilance, anxiety, depression, numbness, dissociation, and sleep deprivation. In particular, what is labeled Religious Trauma Syndrome (RTS) is explicitly tied to authoritarianism coupled with toxic theology.[1] It is my earnest hope and prayer that the prescription asserted in this modest book will bring a source of healing to some of these religious wounds.

---

[1] Downie, Alison. (2022). "Christian Shame and Religious Trauma." RELIGIONS 13(10), 925. www.mdpi.com/2077-1444/13/10/925

I'm currently in my year of Jubilee being a witness to PTCD, which means I've lived fifty years of church ministry and have seen, experienced, and caused hurt in people's lives as a result of conversations, decisions, actions, and failures. Here's the bottom line: God is good and people are not good. People are broken and messy. Jesus isn't messy. Jesus is perfect. Broken people go to church and the Church is filled with broken people who are hoping to heal. The Church isn't broken, people are broken and Jesus is good and perfect. People criticize the Church and Jesus because people are broken. It is sort of like criticizing a hospital because it's filled with sick people. At the hospital, you hope to get well, but some people take time to heal. Sadly, some people don't heal and even get worse. Yes, we might expect more from people who are hoping to get better in the Church, but broken people may take time, and others may get worse. But God is still good. The Church is still good. And people still need Jesus.

I believe I've pinpointed when these types of PTCD messy experiences started happening in the Church. I'm fairly convinced that it all started shortly after the church began. For sure things were heating up in Acts 5 and again in Acts 6, but more than likely pimples in the church were emerging even before then. I'm confident in my assumptions based on my studies of the major themes of the New Testament epistles. If one takes an objective review of the New Testament letters, one will discover that the major themes of the Apostles' letters were about right theology and problems in the church. Paul discussed these conflicts in the early assemblies in Romans through Philemon. I don't even need to try to make a case for Hebrews through Jude, as those God-inspired writings are filled with problems and conflicts between the beautiful people who make up the body of Christ.

It is somewhat of an antinomy to pin down the prayer of Jesus for unity in John 17 and the reality of church history. (If "antinomy" is a new concept to the reader, I invite you to borrow a copy of my previous book where I discuss it a lot since it's a favorite word for me to escape having to answer the hard questions in the Bible). Jesus prayed that God's people would be one as He and the Father are one. I'm confident that Jesus was praying the will of God, but what happened, is happening, and will happen again until the culmination of human history's hot mess, is that God is redeeming it all. Actually, I can go well beyond the early church to the history of God choosing a special people through whom to make Himself known. Okay, it goes further back to Genesis 3 where sin entered the human race.[2]

Here's my quick synopsis of the brokenness of human history as I borrow some thoughts from my wife's book, *Get Out of Control*. We find in Genesis Chapters 1-2, that humanity was created in God's image, and Adam and Eve lived in harmony with God and each other. This is what I call the "true self." It is who God intended us to be. Love, trust, mutuality, friendship, security, and intimacy were

---

[2] Just reflecting on the lineage of the Messiah, Jesus Christ, is enough to display the glory of God's ways in the midst of human brokenness. We only need to read the first chapter of Matthew's Gospel, where we discover the genealogical records of Perez, Rahab, Ruth, and Bathsheba that are filled with failure and scandal while fulfilling God's ultimate redemption.

meant to be dominant in the human experience. But sadly, Chapter 3 of Genesis entered into our narrative. It was there that the "fallen self" was governed by sin, death, blame, shame, and pride. And as a failure result of our fallen human nature, sin multiplies as we interact with others, hurting and wounding more people by the moment. This becomes the realm where fear, errant identities, lies, toxic thoughts, and demonic influences disrupt our love and unity. At this point, it is natural for wounded individuals to self-protect in order to avoid further trauma. Sadly, however, we often use unhealthy coping mechanisms to guard against being hurt any further.

My "pseudo-self" assumed the protective mantle of humor. After an embarrassing incident in my sixth-grade class, I would do anything to get a laugh. I realized that if I could get people to laugh *with* me, I wouldn't necessarily feel that they were laughing *at* me. I became the class clown, so much so, that I earned that superlative in my high school senior yearbook. But deep inside, I was still an insecure eleven-year-old who hid his pain behind a mask of humor. Countless stories replicate this narrative—it isn't special or unique in any way. Young, insecure, and vulnerable children, teenagers, and adults walk through social situations like this every day. Do you remember what it was like to be *that* person who was the brunt of another's cruel comment? Your first experience with woundedness may not have been rejection from a friend. It may have been caused by your parents' divorce, someone else's rage, your older brother's drug addiction, or the death of a loved one that left you feeling lost, lonely, confused, unwanted, and fearful. Not all of us walk away with deep wounds from these types of incidents, but many of us often do. Wounds can trigger us throughout our lives, consciously or unconsciously, due to early experiences of rejection. Insecurity, fear, pain, and uncertainty can rule our interactions with others, and guardedness becomes our default. From our earliest years, at our core we need love and safety for relational security and trust to grow. When love and safety are deprived in our development, rage, shame, control, and chaos can dominate as we are rewired to self-protect. We find ourselves in everyday situations at work, home, or social settings, and of course church, unaware of the fact that we are attempting to control the environment and/or situation we are in. And we're doing it all in a subconscious effort to protect ourselves from wounds inflicted long ago. Rage, shame, control, and/or chaos tell us that self-protection is the safest place to hide and that we have to stay on the defensive, even when doing so traps the controller in a cold and lonely existence. Our wounds push others away and subconsciously create barriers to guard against potential pain. We avoid vulnerability and seek to manipulate others in an effort to shut down every potential offender. These triggers tell us that this is a much easier path than dealing with more pain and that by manipulating situations, circumstances, and relationships, we can have the upper hand. Isolation and withdrawal are its rearguards. Pride is its shield. In its defensiveness, our past tells us the lie that we can't trust anybody but ourselves. We might find ourselves saying, "I'm fine, I'll do it myself. I don't need anybody."

This tragedy has carried on through human history, thus needing Divine redemption. The entire narrative of the Bible reveals repetitive stories of broken and fallen people calling upon God for salvation as He restores our lives to His intended design. It is truly remarkable that none of the heroes of the Bible can take any of the credit or glory. The pages of Scripture are filled with testimonies of God doing glorious things through very fallible vessels. The intention of this modest book is to take a plunge into the deep end of this mysterious tension.

Lastly, some have said that the Church is like a good sausage. It may taste really good, but if you knew what was in it and how it was made, you would never touch it, let alone take a bite. I hope that by the end of this book, we'll be able to enjoy a wonderful knockwurst sandwich together, while knowing fully what is in it, and savoring God's grace and love in the midst of our malaise.

As an addendum to my Preface, my extended friendships may be puzzled by referring to my wife "Marié." My wife of forty-three years is Karen Marié Stonier. What's up with her middle name, Marié? You see, during the crazy COVID season, "Karens" became a bad thing. When we heard about that, I told my wife that she was the furthest thing from one of those "Karens." We agreed on that day to go with her middle name, to which she affirmed that she actually never liked her first name. For the record, I was married to a Karen for forty years, but I just have to say that these past three years, my marriage with Marié has been blissful (as were the previous forty years). For clarification, in case you're confused about this narrative, my entire marriage to Karen Marié Stonier has been heaven on earth. However, we too have lived through the impacts of PTCD and we are alive and well to help others with a prescription for healing from church hurt.

At the end of this booklet you will find reflection questions for life application as an individual or for groups. In addition, there are blank pages wherein you can record your notes and personal commitments for growth.

Chapter One
Ministry Behind the Veil

> "Expect to suffer. Through many tribulations we must enter the kingdom (Acts 14:22)—and the ministry. There are things you cannot know without suffering. God has special tutorials in tribulation for his shepherds. Do not begrudge the seminars of suffering. His aim is to make you, like Jesus, a sympathetic shepherd. It's scary."[3]

Life is often unfair. As a result, there is a danger of becoming polluted by self-centered bitterness. When faced with injustice, God's prescript is to keep our eyes fixed on Him. The mystery and beauty of the Old Testament narrative is alive with lessons and illustrations for personal instruction and reflection. In my years of ministry, I have found great benefit from the wisdom revealed behind the veil of Israel's temple worship. I invite you to take a journey in the shadows of the Old Testament high priests as they approached God within the sacred place of veneration and awe.

---

[3] Mathis, David and Parnell, Jonathan. (2014). *How to Stay Christian in Seminary.* Crossway Books: Wheaton, Illinois p. 13. Forward by John Piper.

After years of intense training and preparation, it was with great anticipation that the new high priest would enter the Holy of Holies to sprinkle the blood of the sacrifice on the mercy seat above the Ark of the Covenant. He knew well what to expect through the rigors of his diligent studies before entering into the temple of God. His predecessors and mentors had labored for years to make sure he was equipped to conduct every nuance of his duties. In this cube-shaped room behind the veil he would see the golden floor and walls, the Ark of the Covenant, and the two cherubim of beaten gold facing the mercy seat. Testifying to a miraculous history, inside the ark contained the tablets of stone given to Moses, a jar of manna, and the rod of Aaron. Only once a year, on the Day of Atonement, one human being was allowed to humbly enter the Most Holy Place. With great reverence and wonder the high priest would be privileged to venture into this sacred domain having passed through a consecrated fragrance of incense reserved only for God. The entire experience would be a hallowed time of ministry wholly to the Lord. The human benefit—atonement for sin—would need to be repeated annually.[4]

---

[4] For a study of prominent Scriptures related to the Biblical ministry behind the veil, see: Exodus 26:33-36; 28:29-43; 29:13-22; 30:6, 20-37; 36:35; 37:1-29; 39:25; 40:1-38; Leviticus 16:2-6, 17-34; 24:3-9; Numbers 4:5;1 Kings 6:1-38; Mark 15:38; Hebrews 9:1-10.

On the high priest's head was a turban and a gold plate held by a blue cord that was engraved with the words "Holiness to the Lord." Upon the hem of his garment were golden bells that "will be heard when he goes into the holy place before the Lord and when he comes out, that he may not die."[5] The intricate particulars of both the attire and the ministry duties were laid out in minute detail that the priests "do not incur iniquity and die. It shall be a statute forever to him and his descendants after him."[6] The role of high priest afforded great honor and responsibility and demanded much piety, but at the same time it came with great trepidation.

One can only imagine the restlessness of that fateful morning when the day dawned for the high priest to fulfill this venerable duty. He had been warned that sometimes people die behind the veil. Perhaps with a spirit overflowing with worship and gratitude, or maybe a mind gripped with anxiety and apprehension, he would press forward cautiously moving through the very thick blue, purple, and

---

[5] Exodus 28:35 (NKJV).
[6] Exodus 28:43 (NKJV).

scarlet veil hung from twenty cubits above by golden clasps. From his reading of the Scriptures, it is quite probable that his imagination would have danced with the expectation of visions of the glimmering gold and the grandeur of God's glorious presence that would light up the Holy of Holies. Very mindful that his heart needed to be aligned in prayer with pure motives and reverence toward such a majestic moment, a host of emotions and excitement would most likely surge like a flood through his entire being. With a wisp of grace, the curtain would close behind him, and now for the very first time he would peer into the place to which his whole life was committed. And what would his gaze behold? Would it be the brilliance of gold reflections splashing from wall to wall and upon the Ark of the Testimony and the mercy seat awaiting his atoning work? I submit that what his senses would drink in at that very instant would be a startling contrast to what his mind had envisioned. With great respect, I suggest that the reality of this most holy environment was aged by centuries of dust, dried blood, and unpolished angelic hosts. There were likely cobwebs and many spiders scurrying about within this secured chamber, startled by this privileged intruder. It is feasible that his mind would have been confused as he got a whiff of stagnant, musty air and that his vision would gaze upon the Ark and mercy seat now layered with cracked, dirty-brown, dried blood. There had been centuries of ceremonies where layers upon layers of atoning blood would have been splattered on the floor and altar. Since the decree was that only the high priest entered this domain once a year, it is very unlikely that a cleaning service ventured behind the veil to polish and clean this inner sanctum. While careful to maintain a sense of wonder, and guarding his heart from doubt or disrespect, the priest's spirit might gasp and whisper, "This is it? This is the Holy of Holies?" I can imagine his hand jerking up quickly to cover his mouth to refrain from further utterances of dismay, his emotions transitioning from fear and awe to a surge of reservation and perhaps even skepticism. The mystery of this moment is shared by many, who tread down a path where expectations of beauty and wonder are displaced by the harsh realities of a broken world. Many God-honoring servants, with the most divine intentions, face this same challenge when they are frustrated by the stains of human failures, injustices, and deceits from the inner workings of the church and its leaders. This is the ministry behind the veil and a contributor to the concept of PTCD. No less startling is the similar trek made by countless others who have ventured behind the veil of contemporary ministry, where their expected visions of the divine were replaced by the very real experiences of tainted, musty, and fractured humanity. It is that first occurrence when an energetic new ministry volunteer or a staff member witnesses a leader's sinful motive or attitude that gives birth to a seed of misperception and eventual criticism. Or it is the newlywed who after months of anticipated joy for marital bliss is awakened to the reality of conflict, dissension, and strange noises and smells. For others it is the longed-for career advancement that erupts with increased stresses and diminished rewards. In my own years of family and ministry, I have witnessed vainglory, narcissism, nepotism, covetousness, abusive authority, prideful motives, and graceless expectations—and these are just the shadows that I see in my own sinister flesh. I have learned that these same character flaws, when shown by others, are a quick excuse for me to displace my critical judgment onto them. It is amazing when I turn my head to squint at the slivers in the eyes of these offenders, how people have to jump aside to avoid being smacked by the plank protruding from my own eye! Yet it is this daily walk behind the many veils of human disappointments that confronts us with our own frailty and our desperate need for grace.

I invite you to take a brief journey with me behind the veils of your life experiences as you reflect on your own wounds and disappointments. But take warning at the outset: there is a great temptation to feel victimized as you feel the burning of injustice in your heart. You will be reminded of little arrows of indiscretion, fraud, and depravity that have pierced your soul over the years and have perhaps blurred the vision of God's glory in the midst of human brokenness. Let God's goodness, mercy, compassion, and love be the guiding light that chaperons your steps on this path behind the veil. And may you experience the Spirit's illumination that transforms pain into purity, mourning into dancing, and bitterness into forgiveness and freedom.

Chapter Two
Two Deadly Questions

> Irving Berlin who lived to be 101, was a Russian Jewish immigrant who wrote approximately 1,500 songs including, "God Bless America" and "White Christmas." Irving Berlin affirmed, when life is faced with challenges, the question is, "Are you going to be a crabby old man or are you going to write another song?"

I have learned in my fifty-year journey with Jesus that there are two deadly questions we should never ask in ministry—although they are two of the most common questions that seem to come like a drizzle upon our minds nearly every day. They are subtle questions, yet they are the very thoughts and words that have pierced through so many hearts to give birth to resentment, bitterness, and pride. I find these questions to be like nettles in my brain, pricking my thoughts when the injustices of others intrude into my world. And it is when our souls are frustrated that these two questions seem to bleed upon those around us, potentially polluting an entire family or community. Even the greatest of saints were not immune to these tempting morsels of misguided utterances. It is the Apostle Peter who asked the first question:

> "Peter, seeing him, said to Jesus, 'But Lord, what about this man?' Jesus said to him, 'If I will that he remain till I come, what is that to you? You follow Me.'"[7]

Question one: "What about him (or her or them)?" When we really stop and contemplate all that God has done to forgive us of our sins, it is stunning. We deserve eternal separation from our Holy God because of our rebellion against Him. And yet, God loved us so much He sent Jesus into the world to pay the debt for our sin. Although we are forgiven and in relationship with God, we still find in our hearts a menacing prompting of the flesh to judge and condemn others for *their* sins.

Jesus told an astute parable about the unforgiving servant. The servant was forgiven of millions of dollars that he owed but wouldn't forgive his debtor of just a few bucks.[8] Why is it that our sins look so much worse on others? When dealing with our own failures, self-reflection and self-awareness are often blinded by pride to avoid acknowledging of our weaknesses.

---

[7] John 21:21-22 (NKJV).
[8] Matthew 18:21-35.

One evening after work, my wife and I walked on the beach. These are always such special times as we get to catch up on things and share about our day's activities. On this particular occasion, I was bothered by a situation where there were a number of injustices and favoritisms amongst the church staff that had been made apparent. As I started to spew my criticism, my wife quickly brought me back down off my high horse and said, "Honey, you follow Jesus." What was comical was that the very next morning, a pastor friend (who wasn't aware of my struggle) relayed to me that he and his wife had gone on a walk the night before where he was stewing over the very same thing I was. His wife in similar fashion cut him off in the middle of his tirade and simply told him to keep his eyes on Jesus. It is God's grace that these two saintly women didn't get pulled into the cesspool of their husbands' emerging bitterness, but instead they gently guided us back in line through Jesus' tender words of correction, "You follow Me."[9]

---

[9] John 21:22 (NKJV).

It is no secret that the husband often sees himself as the head of the house, while the wife is the neck, always turning the head back in the right direction.[10]

There are many times when life and ministry seem unfair, yet I'm often reminded of God's encouragement through the prophet Ezekiel where we learn that His ways are not unfair, but it is our ways that are unfair.[11] God's ways are so far above our ways, and His thoughts are far above our thoughts.[12] We are so limited in our perspectives in life's circumstances. In truth, only the omniscient and omnipresent God has all the facts.

Even King David realized that many of life's challenges were beyond his comprehension. When David penned Psalm 131, I can only imagine that he also struggled with the injustices of life. I get the sense that David humbly learned that his perspective, even as king, was limited, and that he needed to entrust all judgments to the Lord:

---

[10] I would imagine that it was the Apostle Peter's wife that helped him get on track as well. Peter's wife ministered by his side (1 Corinthians 9:5). Clement of Alexandria reports that Peter's wife was martyred before him, and that the apostle encouraged her as she was led to her death with the words, "Follow thou Christ." (Anti Nicene Father Clement ANF 2.541, c. 195) Perhaps it was her example that prepared the apostle for his eventual fulfillment of Jesus' prophetic words in John 21:18-19.
[11] Ezekiel 18:25.
[12] Isaiah 55:7-9. It is important to note the context of these verses, as the eternal mysteries of God's ways and thoughts are the fact that He is merciful and gracious to sinful and rebellious humanity.

> "LORD, my heart is not haughty, nor my eyes lofty. Neither do I concern myself with great matters, nor with things too profound for me. Surely, I have calmed and quieted my soul, like a weaned child with his mother; like a weaned child is my soul within me."[13]

What peace we have when we come to the conclusion that some things are perhaps too high for us, and we can commend these frustrations to the Lord. When you feel your heart surge to burst forth with the question, "What about…?" let the Holy Spirit quiet your soul as you trust Him to make things right—and then simply follow Jesus.

It was Baruch, who penned Jeremiah's prophesies, who asked the second deadly question. Speaking personally to Baruch in response to his self-interest, God warned:

"And do you seek great things for yourself? Do not seek them; for behold, I will bring adversity on all flesh."[14]

---

[13] Psalm 131:1-2 (NKJV).
[14] Jeremiah 45:5 (NKJV). It is interesting to note that God was speaking to Baruch through Jeremiah, but Baruch was given the honor to write his own rebuke in the pages of Scripture.

Question two: "What about me?" In reality, this question is really the same as the first but asked from a subtle root of pride. It is not as overt in attacking others, but is instead the perverse poison of promoting oneself: "What about my needs?" "What's in it for me?" "Why didn't I get...?" In response to our query, God sighs, "Do you seek great things for yourself? Do not seek them."[15]

Though asked in a variety of ways, this folly comes down to the same self-centered core where sin is birthed. Even Satan's fall originated in the assertion, "I will!" "I will ascend into heaven; I will exalt my throne above the stars of God; I will also sit on the mount of the congregation on the farthest sides of the north; I will ascend above the heights of the clouds; I will be like the Most High."[16] Some call it egocentrism. Others call it narcissism. These are both variant terms describing the extremely destructive reality of pride and self-protection. It is this very issue that corrupts a leader. It is this seemingly chronic trait that dissolves families. It is disguised and covered up by many other vices, but ultimately it is sin at its root.

---

[15] Jeremiah 45:5 (NKJV).
[16] Isaiah 14:13-14 (NKJV).

But what is God's heart towards the darkness of people's hearts? Is He full of wrath and fury? Is He strategically waiting for a time to annihilate the filth of His creation? Consider God's perspective when He sees a wayward life:

> "I was crushed by their adulterous heart which has departed from Me, and by their eyes which play the harlot after their idols; they will loathe themselves for the evils which they committed in all their abominations. And they shall know that I am the LORD."[17]

It breaks God's heart that such a self-centered perspective leads people to self-loathing and separation from all the blessings that God had intended for them.[18]

These two questions easily surge to the forefront of our motives when we're befuddled with the troublesome circumstances that invade our lives. The temptation, so subtle and often unnoticed, is to blurt out: "What about him/her?" "What about me?" or "This is unfair!" When this dark, enticing cloud comes upon you, simply pray, "I will follow Jesus!" Always LOOK UP as opposed to looking at

---

[17] Ezekiel 6:9-10 (NKJV).
[18] Matthew 6:33.

others and yourself. When your eyes are on Him, your soul will be quieted and your heart will find a place of perfect peace:

> "You will keep him in perfect peace, whose mind is stayed on You, because he trusts in You. Trust in the LORD forever, for in YAH, the LORD, is everlasting strength."[19]

Have you ever noticed that sorrow, regret, and guilt are birthed from *looking back*, that worry and anxiety come from *looking ahead*, that doubt and despair result from *looking around at the circumstances*, but it is faith that *looks UP*? My wife once again turned my head (which she does quite often) to notice a friend's Facebook post that is quite relevant here, "Yesterday is a canceled check, tomorrow is a promissory note and today is cash in hand. Spend it wisely."[20] And may I pointedly notify you of the huge debit on your account to remind you that life is not about you; it is about Him. To help keep me on

---

[19] Isaiah 26:3-4 (NKJV).
[20] Art Rust, Jr. signed off his WABC (New York City) sports talk radio show with: "Yesterday is a canceled check. Tomorrow is just a promissory note. Today is the only time we have, so spend it wisely. Goodnight, Edna baby." (Rust's wife, Edna, died in 1986, after which he began this signoff.) "'Tomorrow' is a promissory note without a date" is cited in print by at least 1916, written by Henry Kaufman. A more complete version was printed in 1922: "Today is all you have. Tomorrow is a promissory note, and yesterday is a cancelled check. Act Today!" The author of the full phrase is unknown, but it's been credited to George Bernard Shaw, Hubert Tinley and Kay Lyons.

track, I try to remind myself often that we are all family in Christ. And as family, this anacronym has helped me to keep focused: **F.A.M.I.L.Y.**

Forget **A**bout **M**e **I** **L**ove **Y**ou

When tempted to assert one of those two deadly questions, halt and ask another question: "How can I better love God and others?" Love never fails. When injustice happens—love. When your needs are overlooked—love. Truly our *uplook* determines our *outlook*—but oftentimes the pain of being sharply poked makes us want to close our eyes altogether.

A beautiful resolve to this dilemma is found in the footsteps of Jesus. Once again I ask you venture past the veil and to allow God to put your ego on the altar of His grace as you engage actively in the Lord's healing. It is there that you will hurt badly and yet love deeply. It is there that the two self-asserting questions that spring from personal injustice or indignation will dissolve within the ultimate question, "What about Jesus?"

Chapter Three
With-ness Empowers Witness

> "God didn't make a contract with us; God made a covenant with us, and God wants our relationships with one another to reflect that covenant. That's why marriage, friendship, life in community are all ways to give visibility to God's faithfulness in our lives together."[21]

One of the most cherished joys in my life is to be on vacation with my entire family. I love our shared meals, stories, laughter, activities, games, and faith discussions. When our kids and grandkids are all together, it's a slice of heaven for my wife and me. On one of our recent getaways, after an evening dinner, we gathered in a circle as Boppa (my preferred nickname) led our clan in a conversation about the main themes of the Scriptures. I posed the question, "Besides the obvious answer of *Jesus,* what is one word that you would use to summarize the message of the entire Bible?" Each family member paused to reflect, and then one by one they each shared their word. In sequence, the beautiful concepts of love, grace, relationship, hope, salvation, etc. were declared with gratefulness. At the end of

---

[21] Nouwen, Henri. (2006). *Bread for the Journey: A Daybook of Wisdom and Faith.* HarperOne: New York: NY.

our family circle, I asserted my word, "with." We all chuckled when my wife questioned why I chose such a simple preposition. "With?" It's perhaps not as dynamic as the other great words that were chosen, but for me it's a word that captures the heart of the Bible. Maybe I cheated a little, since I couldn't use Jesus as my word, but instead chose being *with* Jesus.

Throughout the Bible we learn that in times of blessings and in times of challenge, God is always present, making Himself known. God's covenant of grace is one of relationship where we become His people and He becomes our God.[22] And within this covenantal relationship the Lord wants us to know His ever-present help in times of need.[23] It is in His presence that we can experience

the fullness of joy and life as God makes Himself known in every situation. It was during the plagues in Egypt and other national events that God's people would know that YHWH is God and that

He would always be with them.[24] The Lord promised to make Himself

---

[22] Exodus 6:2-7.
[23] "God *is* our refuge and strength, a very present help in trouble" (Psalm 46:1 NKJV).
[24] YHWH is a form of the Hebrew name of God used in the Bible. YHWH was traditionally a name too sacred to be uttered, and therefore, without vowels the sound of God's name is uncertain. See Exodus 6:7; 14:4, 18; Ezekiel 5:13, 6:7-14. In Ezekiel this declaration is repeated throughout the book over seventy times, primarily in relation to judgment.

known through His fulfilled promises and blessings.[25]

Many are perhaps familiar with the Messianic Scripture: "Therefore the Lord Himself will give you a sign: behold, the virgin shall conceive and bear a Son, and shall call His name Immanuel."[26] Immanuel means "God *with* us!" What an amazing concept! The God of the universe desires to have a relationship *with* us through His beloved Son. Isaiah 7:14 possibly conjures up thoughts of Christmas or maybe a childhood memory of an old Sunday school felt-board story. However, these wonderful memories can be in danger of drifting into an idle place of empty tradition and religious familiarity. People can end up missing one of the most dynamic and intimate revelations from the very heart of God.

I believe that one of the greatest challenges to an authentic relationship with God is the slumber of empty religion. By that, I mean to define religion as a set of customs and rituals that are externally experienced by many who only have a casual, mental

---

[25] Exodus 10:3; 16:6, 12; 29:46; 31:13; Deuteronomy 29:6; Joshua 3:10; 4:24; Ezekiel 16:62.
[26] Isaiah 7:14 (NKJV).

acknowledgment of God's existence. Individuals can slip into a dreary routine of occasional church attendance, lacking a genuine, deep, abiding relationship *with* Jesus Christ. How grateful we should be to know and enjoy God and the intimate communion He longs to have with us. He simply wants to be *with* us and to transform us into the likeness of His Son. On the other hand, there is that dangerous place where people take part in a religion that tries to work its way into God's acceptance, living under a sense of obligation, guilt, and shame.

I've heard people often state that Christianity isn't a religion, but rather, it is a relationship. I don't disagree with this; however, I would like to propose that it's more than this. You see, a person can have a relationship with their barista wherein they know each other's names and preferred coffee request, but they don't know anything deeper or more personal about each other's lives. Similarly, many religious people can know things *about* God but never really *know* Him intimately and personally – which, by the way, is where the fun begins with God. Sometimes people displace intimacy *with* God by focusing on their service *to* God. One's identity in being a dearly loved son or daughter of God can be easily lost in our ministry activity. Serving others is a blessing, but not at the expense of neglecting time at Jesus' feet.[27]

From Genesis to Revelation, the Bible consistently reveals that the Lord desires to be *with* us. In the Garden of Eden, God sought to be *with* Adam and Eve as He walked in the cool of the day.[28] In Revelation, God's tabernacle is "*with* men and He will dwell *with* them and they shall be His people, God Himself will be *with* them and be their God."[29] For me the Bible can be summed up as a narrative of the eternal, omnipotent God creating the entire universe for His glory, and at the heart of His purposes is His desire to be in intimate relationship *with* His people. It was in another garden—Gethsemane—that Jesus prayed for our union and oneness that parallels the oneness of marriage, "that they may be one just as We are one: I in them, and You in Me; that they may be made perfect

---

[27] And of course Luke 10:38-42 gives us acute insight into this very essential dynamic.
[28] Genesis 3:8.
[29] Revelation 21:3 (NKJV) emphasis mine.

in one, and that the world may know that You have sent Me, and have loved them as you have loved Me."[30] As Jesus proclaimed the Great Commission to His disciples, He promised, "I am *with* you always, even to the end of the age."[31] And not only does Jesus long to be *with* us, Scripture reveals that God is *for* us, *in* us, and that He seeks to come *upon* us in His fullness.[32] Knowledge of this divine intention of relationship sets us free from the burden of compulsory religion. No matter what life throws at us, God longs for us to know that He is with us to deliver us; it is then that we shall know that YHWH is God.[33]

I've come to learn in my own journey of faith that the more I abide in the presence of God, the more dynamic my witness is. Thus, our "with-ness" is what truly empowers our witness. Jesus asserted in John 15:5, "I am the vine, you are the branches. He who abides in Me, and I in him, bears much fruit; for without Me you can do nothing." Our fruitfulness is directly correlated with our with-ness, and my

---

[30] John 17:22-23 (NKJV).
[31] Matthew 28:20 (NKJV) emphasis mine. For other "with" themes see: Genesis 28:15, 31:3, 46:4; Exodus 3:12; Deuteronomy 31:8, 23; Joshua 1:5, 9; Judges 6:12; 1 Samuel 10:7; 1 Kings 8:57; 1 Chronicles 28:20; 2 Chronicles 1:1, 20:17; Psalm 23:4, 118:6; Isaiah 41:10, 43:2, 5; Jeremiah 1:8, 19, 15:20, 20:11, 42:11, 46:28; Ezekiel 43:9; Haggai 1:13, 2:4; Zechariah 8:23, 10:5; Matthew 1:23, 18:20; Hebrews 13:5.
[32] Psalm 56:9; Romans 8:31; Ephesians 3:17; Colossians 1:27; Isaiah 59:21; Acts 1:8, 10:44, 11:15, 19:6.
[33] See Joshua 1:9, 3:7; Jeremiah 1:8, 19, 16:21.

fleshliness erupts when I neglect His presence. The fruit, power, and gifts of the Holy Spirit flow from being connected to the Vine—our sole Source of love, power, and the abundant life.

Behind the veil of ministry, many of God's people are busy being about the *work* of God, while neglecting the *Word* of God. In my doctoral dissertation survey work, I discovered that pastors often replace daily devotional study with sermon preparation; justifying to ourselves that, "after all, we're *still* studying the Bible." But there's a difference between intimate, abiding *communion* with God and preparing to tell others *what* the Bible teaches. Similarly, studies on pastoral ministry have shown that church leaders communicate strongly to their congregations about the importance of being accountable in a small group, while pastors tend to be the worst offenders in regard to being held accountable by others.[34] The demands of ministry and everyday life can easily influence leaders to displace the important with the urgent, which often leads to a very

---

[34] Kinnaman, G. and Ells, A. (2003). *Leaders That Last: How Covenant Friendships Can Help Pastors Thrive.* Baker Books, Grand Rapids, MI.

anemic spiritual life. "Fake it until you make it" may be a work ethic for some, but in the ministry, faking it is a fatal flaw to authentic, fruitful faith.

One Sunday while serving at my church, I made an intentional effort to really slow down and engage people personally to ask how they were doing. Halfway through the morning I was astounded to hear how so many people replied to my inquiry with the same word: "busy." I was reminded of a passage in Eugene Peterson's book, *The Contemplative Pastor,* where he sharply

warned, "The word *busy* is the symptom not of commitment but of betrayal. It is not devotion but defection. The adjective *busy* set as a modifier to *pastor* should sound to our ears like *adulterous* to characterize a wife or *embezzling* to describe a banker. It is an outrageous scandal, a blasphemous affront."[35] And please know, I'm not trying to point out the sins and neglect of others, as I have been the worst offender in my ministry pursuits early in my calling.

---

[35] Peterson, Eugene. (1989). *The Contemplative Pastor: Returning to the Art of Spiritual Direction.* Eerdmans Publishing: Grand Rapids, MI.

Years ago, a police officer shared the story about pulling over a traffic offender for doing a "California stop" and rolling through a stop sign. When he approached the driver, the officer was met with resistance as the person argued that he had at least slowed down. "But the sign says, 'STOP'" came the reply. The driver argued further until the officer started to tap him repeatedly on the head with his pen. "What are you doing? Stop that!" huffed the driver. To which the officer replied, "Do you want me to slow down or stop?" Maybe I'm stretching this point a little far, but sometimes the Lord has had to metaphorically tap me on the head to get me not just to slow down but to stop what I'm doing and return to my first love.

Behind the veil can be a very busy place. And this is fine when the fruit of the Spirit is dominant—love, joy, peace, longsuffering, kindness, goodness, faithfulness, gentleness, and self-control should be abounding. But when conflict, strife, criticism, judgment, and anger are dominant, slow down and then stop to consider the Lord's nudging to refocus on Jesus. Sometimes post-traumatic church disorder is the result of a busy group of individuals bumping into each other as they are "serving Jesus." When our *worth* is attached to our *work*, and our work is powered by the flesh and not the Spirit, people get hurt. Truly our growth in being a witness will be impacted greatly by our devotion to with-ness.

    I was once visiting a church that had the sign displayed, "Mission First, People Always." This is a nice statement, but even better should be, "People First, Mission Always." When we are abiding in Jesus Christ we will be more intentional in loving people well, while on mission. Sadly, a gifted leader can be misguided to see people as a means to an end in accomplishing a mission. God's blueprint is that people *are* the mission. Personally, I see this misplaced priority as being somewhat demonic. That may seem to be a harsh statement until we realize that one of the devil's main schemes is to use and manipulate humans to accomplish his goal of dethroning God. When leaders begin to treat people harshly and become somewhat abusive in pushing the masses toward *their* goals, the casualties of post-traumatic church disorder will be the fruit. And God wants better for His people. God wants a culture of love to be pervasive in all that is done. After all, God is love.[36]

---

[36] 1 John 4:7-8.

Chapter Four
Embitterment Disorder

"You can easily tell when someone has been hit by a spear. He turns a deep shade of bitter. David never got hit. Gradually, he learned a very well-kept secret. He discovered three things that prevented him from ever being hit. One, never learn anything about the fashionable, easily mastered art of spear throwing. Two, stay out of the company of all spear throwers. And three, keep your mouth tightly closed. In this way, spears will never touch you, even when they pierce your heart."[37]

The domains of faith, family, and friends are supposed to be places of safety and refuge. But for many, these sacred places are the means by which people have been most severely violated. Our home and our place of worship should be communities of security, protection, and growth. Yet there are countless tales where these revered sanctuaries have become the means of painful assaults. When the onslaught of injustice originates from those closest to us, the complexities of the resulting pain can become fertile soil for bitterness and hatred.

---

[37] Edwards, Gene. (1980). *A Tale of Three Kings: A Study in Brokenness.* Seedsowers Publishing: Newnan, GA. p. 19-20.

Where do we turn when the sacred foundations of love and mercy have crumbled? To whom can we go for perspective and understanding? How can we overcome such surmounting obstacles to return to the realm of *normal?* Can *normal* even be a reality for us again? Some of life's darkest and most horrific circumstances can challenge one's faith to question if certain situations can ever be redeemed on this side of eternity. Yet, when we rest in the fact that God is sovereign and is at work to redeem the most tragic of losses, we are assured that all will be reconciled, even if the timing isn't until we are with Him in heaven.

When we add to these challenges the stumbling block of hypocrisy and betrayal at one's church or home, the heart, mind, and soul can be sent spinning in innumerable directions. These offenses can blind a person from an upward gaze of God's grace to be locked onto the failures and carnality of others. This becomes a cancerous poison that can impact one's heart towards embitterment.

A research study a number of years ago asserted that the mismanagement of injustice can not only lead to you being *dead wrong*, it can also lead you to being *dead*. People with the strongest feelings of being treated unfairly were more than twice as likely to have serious heart disease, heart attacks, or angina in relation to those who seldom deal with injustice at work. Yes, it is unfair when we are treated poorly through inequality and prejudice, and these offensives are just plain wrong. However, when we grow bitter as a result of those inequities, we are further injured through the emotional, mental, and physiological effects of internalized stress. In this way, the person who initially hurt us continues to hurt us through our own internal turmoil.

I refer to these experiences as "toxic thoughts." The fumes of resentment, cynicism, unforgiveness, revenge, grudges, and animosity become venomous to our spirits.[38] The book of Hebrews provides counsel in guarding against bitterness: "Pursue peace with all people, and holiness, without which no one will see the Lord: looking carefully lest anyone fall short of the grace of God; lest any

---

[38] The Apostle Peter warned a man named Simon who was "poisoned by bitterness." See Acts 8:14-25. For an excellent resource on this subject, consider the book by Dr. Caroline Leaf, *Switch on Your Brain: The Key to Peak Happiness, Thinking, and Health*. Baker Books, Grand Rapids, MI, (2013).

root of bitterness springing up cause trouble, and by this many become defiled."[39] In addition, some individuals continue in their bitter torment, even after an antagonist has died. If left unattended, some abuses can continue to reach beyond the grave to assault our hearts as we recall those lethal memories to our own demise.

PTSD is becoming a well-known malady in our modern era. Traumatic events can have long-lasting impairment in people's lives. However, a more recent challenge that many are not aware of is PTED – Posttraumatic Embitterment Disorder. PTED is a type of pathological reaction to adverse life events and is characterized by a distinct psychological process (experiences of injustice and violation of basic beliefs) and by a highly specific psychopathological profile (embitterment and intrusions). PTED manifests in feelings of helplessness, self-blame, suicidal ideation, dysphoria, aggression, down-heartedness, reduced drive, seemingly melancholic depression, unspecific somatic complaints, loss of appetite, sleep disturbances, pain, and phobic symptoms with respect to the place or persons related to the event.[40]

---

[39] Hebrews 12:14-15 (NKJV).
[40] https://www.karger.com/Article/Abstract/70783

Once again it is crucial to understand that when an individual falls into the trap of unforgiveness and bitterness, the hurt individual further harms themselves. This doesn't mean we should be flippant about the injustice and just forgive and forget. After all, forgetfulness is a sign of brain impairment. Forgiveness, on the other hand, is a major component of one's spiritual maturity and discipleship. The Bible repeatedly teaches that we are to forgive as we have been forgiven by God.[41] Essentially, our forgiveness is rooted in our forgiven-*ness*.

Further complicating things is the fact that a person's embittered reactions to offense can often result in further entanglement with unresolved childhood wounds. Over the years, I have observed the truth of the adage, "Hurt people, hurt people." Hurt people often multiply their perspective of the personal injury because it unconsciously gets entangled with previous wounds. Childhood parental abandonment, father absence, neglect, and abuse can sadly echo throughout one's lifetime. These early painful

---

[41] Matthew 6:14-15, 18:21-22; Mark 11:25-26; Luke 6:37-38; Colossians 3:12-13; Ephesians 4:31-32; Psalm 32:1, 86:5.

experiences, when unresolved, ripple through one's life and when later wounds occur, a tidal wave of embitterment emerges.

I have witnessed people launching into a bitter tirade as they poison others with their story of the injustice they have endured, utterly unaware that their pain is actually rooted in childhood trauma. Hurt people often place expectations on others that they wished had been met decades ago by someone other than their targeted offender. Truly, hurt people *do* hurt people. But I have also learned that loved people, love people; encouraged people encourage people; and forgiven people forgive people.

If we neglect forgiveness, embitterment will leak from our hearts into our conversations with others and will further spread the poison. People who have been wounded in relationships will frequently release their pain on others by verbalizing their toxicity. The eruption of slander and the spreading of discord is sadly a normal but dreadful course for embittered souls. It is crucial to recognize that there are demonic forces at work when the tongue pours out slander. In fact, the name "Devil" comes from the Greek word *Diabolos,* meaning "Slanderer." To slander and spread the toxic words from bitterness is literally speaking Satan's language. It is no wonder then, that Proverbs 6:16-19 says that God hates the spreading of discord. In fact, this Scripture reveals seven things that are an abomination before the Lord, and three of the seven have to do with the tongue—yikes!

It may be hard to accept at first impression, but did you know that no one has actually ever died from a poisonous snake bite? It's the venom that kills, not the bite itself. People say and do things that can cause us to hurt, and therein lies the bite. But bitterness is the deadly venom, which stems from our own souls. And forgiveness is the antidote that saves us from ourselves.

A couple in our church experienced the richness of forgiveness from the devastating wound of infidelity. Forgiveness happened through baptism, though not in the manner you might expect. Years ago, the wife discovered the betrayal of her husband.

Through counseling and coming to faith in Christ, their marriage was restored. However, the scars were still an impediment in their marriage, as it often takes time for forgiveness to grow into trust again.

About a decade after her conversion, the wife finally signed up to get baptized on the 10th of June in Mission Bay in San Diego. Her husband was going to join me in baptizing his wife. However, on the morning of the scheduled baptism, his wife woke up angry at her husband. An argument ensued, and in a moment of frustration she decided to put off her baptism yet again. As the day progressed, she spent some time in prayer and the Lord brought to her mind that it was on June 10th ten years earlier that she had discovered her husband's affair. Tears flooded her eyes as the pain of betrayal emerged once again.

In faith, she decided to get baptized that afternoon as originally planned. And when she emerged from the cool bay water, joy filled her heart as she embraced her forgiven husband. She exclaimed that God re-wrote the legacy of June 10th with her baptism. Deep in her subconscious lurked the memory of betrayal that God replaced with the wonder of her baptism. A washing of renewal brought divine healing to a profound wound that had been buried deep in her heart. As the tide went out that evening, sorrow turned to joy, and the new memory of her renewed commitment to Christ set her free from bitterness.

In my own ministry journey, I have been crushed multiple times by the decisions and actions of others I've respected. Once, I was put on display before my peers and falsely accused of wrongdoing. Even after I was vindicated, I still had to wade through the pain of the lack of apologies and righting of wrongs. As a result of these heart-wrenching offenses, I have quit the ministry dozens of times in my heart. Yet, when I bring my open wounds before the Lord in prayer, He shows me His hands and feet. I am reminded of the multitudes shouting, "Crucify Him! Crucify Him!" My cries settle into whimpers, which eventually dissipate when I sense Jesus' embrace. As I abide in the place of God's compassion, a surge of His grace carries me through the valley of the shadow of embitterment. It feels so good to come out the other side and experience the freedom that comes from forgiveness.

Here's the deal: throughout our lives, we run into countless experiences where people and situations upset us. We will experience actions and words that are just flat-out wrong and hurtful. Our natural tendency is to defend ourselves and put people in their place. Many find themselves living in a daily battle, fighting for their rights to maintain the uprightness of their situation and their pursuit of personal happiness. To deal with this temptation, I have found 1 Peter 2:18-25 to be a helpful guide in gaining God's perspective on injustice, as we are encouraged to do what Jesus would do.

Ultimately, walking in Jesus' steps and doing what Jesus did puts us on a course of healing grace. Jesus suffered continual injustices in his short time on earth. He was mocked, lied about, slandered and crucified, and yet He did not retaliate. Instead, Jesus entrusted Himself to His loving Father.

Similarly, our approach should be that no matter how unfair things may seem, we must commit and entrust ourselves "to Him who judges righteously."[42] In other words, we should live with the

---

[42] 1 Peter 2:23 (NKJV).

contentment of knowing that we serve an audience of One. We should thrive with the viewpoint that God sees all, and what matters is that we live in the mindset that God is just and He will work all things according to His perfect will. We can let go of the controls and experience our surrender to His good will and pleasure. Yes, doing so is humbling, but humility was the manner in which Jesus responded to His accusers and assailants. By following His example, we can get in step with His humility and surrender to His Father's higher perspective. In addition, notice that in 1 Peter 3:1, 7, the word "likewise" connects how we relate to one another in marriage. "Likewise," finds its direct context back in 1 Peter 2:23, where couples are challenged to commit themselves "to Him who judges righteously." If you decide to make this perspective the focal point of your relationship with others, you will grow in Christ's likeness in ways that take you to the very cornerstone of your faith.

Moreover, if you live by this precept, you will find that your life aligns with Jesus Christ in just about everything else. However, you will also discover that this can be one of the most difficult places to consistently abide. Christlikeness is a beautiful witness to the brokenness of our hurting world, but it's often borne in the crucible of the Cross. Just as the Cross wasn't fair for Jesus to bear, nor will it be for you. This takes us back to the founding principle of our faith: that the grace we receive from God is fundamentally unfair and thoroughly undeserved.

Chapter Five
Freedom in Forgiveness

"We must develop and maintain the capacity to forgive. He who is devoid of the power to forgive is devoid of the power to love."[43]

In the process of writing this book, I have been a witness to a number of very painful situations that warrant a prescription for healing from church hurt. Recently, I was asked to provide perspective and support to a group of individuals who were struggling over a spiritual mentor who took his life through suicide. What do you say? How do you address this definite betrayal and

inconsistency? I had a few thoughts but was not really settled on how I was going to address this group the next morning. However, God was faithful as He abruptly woke me up at 3:15AM with a Scripture that invaded my dreams. "He who is without sin among you, let him throw a stone."[44] We all have opinions and thoughts

about people's inconsistencies, but we clearly don't possess God's

---

[43] Attributed to Martin Luther King, Jr.
[44] John 8:7 (NKJV)

complete perspective. He alone knows *all* of the facts and He alone has the grace that is sufficient for all circumstances. It is in God that mercy and truth are harmonized: "Mercy and truth have met together; righteousness and peace have kissed."[45] How beautiful it was to see this community of struggling friends grow in grace as we all entrusted ourselves to God who is merciful with the truth.

Oh, how I needed this reminder when a short time after this incident I was confronted with the news of an apparent abusive and insecure pastor who intentionally humiliated a gifted young leader. This was followed by hearing the news of a couple of prominent church leaders having to step down from their ministries due to overt moral failures. It is so easy to assume the worst and rush to judgment, but then again, I heard a whisper saying, "He who is without sin among you…"

How do we balance love and forgiveness with very hurtful duplicity? Loving something or someone necessarily opens our

---

[45] Psalm 85:10 (NKJV)

hearts to the likelihood of being hurt. This does not mean that we should be defenseless against abuse or enable another's bad behavior. It does, however, mean that we have to allow ourselves exposure to potential pain in order to experience true love. Though seemingly paradoxical, vulnerability is a pathway to freedom.

An ally of self-protection and defensiveness is their close cousin, *narcissism.* Narcissism embodies a grandiose sense of self-importance and lacks empathy for others, given its self-focus. But what many fail to recognize is that narcissism stems most often from wounded inner children seeking to guard themselves at all cost. A narcissist's pain prevents them from recognizing his or her own self-focus, skewing their perception of reality. That's why narcissists often identify narcissism in other people, when in fact, they are merely projecting a mirror image of their need to control for the purpose of self-protection. And of course, we all have a tinge of narcissism in us because self-focus is at the center of our fallen human nature. As such, we need to be careful in judging the narcissism in others, since we may be looking into a mirror without even realizing it.

Becoming offended by the injustice of others often causes us to run away from them while peeking in the rearview mirror. The little kid in us hopes that someone cares enough to chase us. Ironically, our wounds can make us afraid of being truly vulnerable, creating a craving for authenticity that eludes us due to our self-created barriers. Offended people want to connect but sabotage their own opportunities to do so. They want to feel safe enough to let go but rarely release the reins enough to see if that's even possible. Hurting people lack trust, which is essential to experiencing true intimacy and love in our closest relationships.

Where lack of trust has been our experience, we tend to cling to control. In order to feel safe, people subconsciously try to reduce their inner anxiety by controlling the people and circumstances around them. Control provides a false security and rarely eliminates anxiety. At the foundation of trust is the need for authentic faith. It seems counterintuitive to controlling people that to experience freedom from the pain of our past, we must give up control. Letting go, being vulnerable, and allowing people to know us requires a huge leap of faith. Faith turns vulnerability into freedom and transforms trust into intimacy.

Don't read on too quickly as this is such an important principle to grasp. Let me repeat: faith turns vulnerability into freedom and transforms trust into intimacy. True freedom is rooted in faith in the God of love. His love and perspective work in us to restore us into our original design of wholeness.

It is at the juncture of injustice, control, vulnerability, and faith where forgiveness unlocks the heart to experience liberty. Our humanity has an inner drive that fights for a sense of fairness. Social research reveals that people tend to relate to one another on a basis of fairness, otherwise known as Social-Equity Theory. Though not always intentional, people will treat others as they have been treated – in other words, the thought process is that "if you are nice to me, then I'll be nice to you." Conversely, "If you are harsh or cruel, then I don't have to be kind to you either." In a naturalistic sense, people tend to relate to one another on a contractual basis. If you hold up your end of the bargain, then I'll hold up mine. A contract upholds justice, but God dealt with us according to His relational covenant of grace. Justice is getting what we deserve and giving it right back. Mercy, on the other hand, is not getting what we deserve. And grace is getting the blessings of even *more* than we deserve.

Studies show that people tend to greatly overestimate the benefits they bestow upon others and underestimate the harm they do to others. We are also inclined to intensify our experience of the pain inflicted upon us by others. These tendencies provide evidence of our fallen human nature, where apart from Christ, we focus our perception from the viewpoint of the self. People generally have a self-centered orientation to the world around them. This becomes the fertile soil where the poison of bitterness can grow deep roots in a person's heart. What people fail to grasp is that bitterness and lack of forgiveness further exasperate one's pain, leading to very dynamic physical, emotional, and spiritual damage.

A few years ago, my son and I booked a lunch date at one of our favorite sushi restaurants. Our conversation ended up going quite deep into some of the painful experiences he had at church growing up. Being a part of a large congregation, with his dad being one of the pastors, can present some unique challenges.[46] He shared about

---

[46] For an academic study of the dynamics of pastoral families, two of my doctoral professors provide some great insights in their work: Lee, Cameron and Balswick, Jack (1989). *Life in the Glass House: The Minister's Family in its Unique Social Context.*

the pressure church leaders would put upon him since he was a "pastor's kid." They expected saintly behavior that even they themselves wouldn't measure up to.

Another challenge he shared was when my son would frequent the homes of some of his buddies, where the parents were quite active in the church. He was regularly conflicted to see first-hand how these adults acted one way at church and then witnessed a dramatic contrast from how they behaved and spoke at home. This of course is understandable, since we all have our failures. As our kids were growing up, we often discussed about how to navigate the humanity of others and ourselves. However, there was one experience that pierced my son's soul deeply, of which I had never heard until that day. His pain was rooted in an encounter with a youth pastor at a youth retreat in the mountains. The church, including youth gatherings, is expected to be hallowed ground for safety and encouragement. But not so on this youth excursion, I would soon learn. The venomous bite occurred on an evening when the pastor was teaching on forgiveness and asked the students to identify someone at the retreat who perhaps had offended them. The assignment was to stoop down, wash the feet of the one who hurt them, and ask for forgiveness. As you might expect from a room full of middle schoolers, no one stepped out to confront a wound. After a time of awkward silence, the youth pastor decided to call my son up on the stage in front of all of his peers.

    Having been a youth pastor for nearly twenty years myself, this scenario brought chills to my heart. Public humiliation can be incredibly damaging for kids, with lasting effects. And, so it was for my son. The leader got down on his knees and began washing my son's feet in front of the entire room of students. Then the fatal blow was inflicted when the youth pastor asked for my son's forgiveness. Kneeling down, the young leader asked for forgiveness as he told my son that he always thought that my son wasn't good enough to have a dad who was a pastor. He then bit harder stating that he didn't think my son deserved the father that he had.

These words had likely come from a deep sense of hurt in this pastor's own life, blinding him to the venom he had injected. The jeering and jokes that later pounced upon my son by his friends were added fuel to disengage him from the church altogether. Reflecting back, I remember a season when it was a battle to get him to go to youth group. Now I knew why and could totally understand the humiliation he endured that impacted his faith for years to come.

Thankfully in the ensuing years my son was able to find forgiveness for this youth pastor. As an adult, my son realized that this leader was young and was perhaps a little overly righteous in his early years of ministry. He was trying to follow Christ's example but was a little insensitive to his audience. In fact, my son has been able to use this story with his own son and daughter, to better equip them on the grace needed for the good intentions that end up feeling like snake bites. That initial nip can hurt, he tells them, but don't let it become deadly. Being quick to forgive is a good antidote for any poison the enemy intends to inject us with. As Nelson Mandela stated so accurately, "Resentment is like drinking poison and then hoping it will kill your enemies."

So, what can we do with this quagmire of pain, injustice, bitterness, and resentment in relation to people who have hurt us? How do we forgive those who have wronged us? Here is a brief encouragement for you to walk through some basic steps for healing that comes from forgiveness.

First, pray for God's grace to empower you to forgive. It isn't natural to forgive; it's divine. We don't have the ability to forgive others within ourselves, but we can be a vessel and a conduit of Jesus' forgiveness shown to us. Some have said that we need to forgive and forget. But as stated earlier, forgetfulness is likelier a sign of brain damage. We are commanded to forgive, through which God provides the strength, power, and healing to follow through with His grace. In relation to being hurt by others, however, it is crucial to remember that forgiveness does NOT mean:

1) They were innocent and are acquitted for their behaviors.
2) That you have to somehow forget what happened.
3) That you have to trust the offender moving forward.
4) That you can't be angry or disturbed by what happened.

In addition, you need to be honest with any anger or bitterness against God for the hurt you've experienced through this person. Ask the Lord to heal your emotions, anger, resentment, and memories caused by the offense. Thank the Lord for understanding your pain and bearing the pain, sin, and shame you've endured. Then give God the right to hold the other individuals accountable for their sin and to bring justice and grace to you. Release yourself from personally trying to get justice and revenge for how you were treated. Allow God to have access to the hurt you experienced so that you can verbally say a Spirit-led prayer to the Lord like this:

> *"In the name of Jesus, I choose to forgive as I have been forgiven. I choose to forgive (<u>name the person</u>) for (<u>name the specific offenses</u>). I release my right to bring revenge. I release them from my hands and let go of all resentment and bitterness. I break and cancel every curse I have expressed and call forth a blessing towards them. Forgive me Lord for any way that I have responded in my pain with sin. I receive your forgiveness and ask for healing in Jesus' name, amen."*

Thank the Lord for the freedom He grants you and the forgiveness He has given you. Thank Jesus for restoring your relationship and right standing with Him.

Oh yeah, one more thing before you move on—go back and re-read the previous paragraph and take a moment to actually engage these encouragements and prayer. It is so easy to merely read and hear about what we should do and to think that this would be a good thing to do someday. *Now* is the time for engaging your total and complete freedom. Get alone in a quiet place where the Holy Spirit will guide you in the liberty He wants for you through forgiveness. You are dearly loved by God and it is His pleasure to bring healing into your life and relationships.

Final Thoughts

"In essentials, unity; in non-essential, liberty; in all things, charity."[47]

Since the two greatest commandments are to love God and to love people, love and compassion for others should be dominant in our interactions, no matter how diverse our opinions may be. Fortunately, the Lord continues to give me ongoing situations where I get the privilege of relearning the precepts of unity, liberty, and charity. Of late, I have observed a number of quick-tempered people who have been swift to criticize, assume, judge, or flat-out blow up over other people's perspectives or efforts. Recently, I even received angry criticism from an individual who was distraught that Bible study software was being promoted at a church service as an effort to help people study the Bible (Really?!). Social media is filled with reactive comments that are saturated with anger, rage, and hatred over differences of opinion. It breaks my heart that we can't pause, listen, and seek to better understand others' perspectives. But then again, we are all victims of our own triggers at times.

---

[47] This widely used quote, is an aphorism variously attributed to St. Augustine of Hippo, German theologian Rupertus Meldenius, German reformer Philip Melanchthon, John Wesley and to a number of other theologians in between them all.

Paul the Apostle often dealt with conflict, and his response to the church in Philippi was, "Whether in pretense or in truth, Christ is preached; and in this I rejoice, yes, and will rejoice."[48] When individuals came to Jesus concerned about others doing things differently, He stated, "Do not forbid him, for he who is not against us is on our side."[49] Now, please hear me; I'm not saying that truth doesn't matter. Paul also wrote, "But even if we, or an angel from heaven, preach any other gospel to you than what we have preached to you, let him be accursed."[50] The virtues of truth and love can at times seem to be in tension with each other. Jesus affirmed that the truth of the Gospel would bring division and offense in some of our relationships.[51] But before reacting to others, we need to hear people out by listening, learning, discerning, understanding, and loving. We must always consider the grace shown to us in Jesus Christ and seek to reflect that grace back to others.

Several years ago, a pastor friend lost his wife of over forty years to a battle with cancer that lasted for close to a decade. A year

---

[48] Philippians 1:18 (NKJV).
[49] Luke 9:50 (NKJV).
[50] Galatians 1:8 (NKJV).
[51] See Matthew 10:34-39.

after his wife died, he remarried a wonderful Christian woman who shared his ministry passions. However, he was attacked by numerous church members and friends believing that he was moving too quickly into this new marriage. First off, his decision to move forward in this relationship was encouraged through prayer and the guidance of trusted mentors. Criticism continued to abound leading to a formal response that actually helped to bring perspective to my own journey of loss. The pastor enlightened his critics by letting them know that for the previous ten years, because of his wife's illness, his role had transitioned into more of a caretaker rather than that of a husband. To outsiders, he had just lost his wife the previous year. But to my friend, he'd lost her nearly a decade earlier.

When I heard this testimony, it brought healing to my heart for the death of my mom when I was twelve years old. She had battled cancer for over four years, and most of my memories were of her hospitalizations and devastating sicknesses. Six months after her passing, my dad let me know that he was going to be marrying a friend who had helped our family through our tough season of bereavement. It was hard for me to accept that my dad was moving on so quickly. I remember my eyes welling up with tears when he shared his intentions with me. So, when I heard my pastor friend's story, it took me back fifty years and helped me realize that my dad's role in my mom's life had changed to a caretaker's role as well. This realization brought a lot of healing along with it.

Human nature tends to react swiftly and defensively to information contrary to how we believe the world should be. Media has capitalized on stirring up people's emotions with morsels of partial reports that ignite our more primitive drives toward rage and indignation. "Clickbait" on the internet entices people to read scandalous stories by sensationalizing and exploiting others to appease the public's curiosity. And the hooks they use generally appeal to our basest responses to different opinions, assumptions, and beliefs. Sadly, the narcissist in all of us believes that we are always right, and our opinions are the most valid.

It's worth noting that it is perfectly normal for individuals to have strong reactions to viewpoints contrary to one's convictions. But rather than allow them to upset us, we should use them to expand our growth toward greater self-reflection and self-awareness. Our emotional maturity grows when we approach things that seem foreign to us through the lens of curiosity, and unearth the source of our discomfort to varying worldviews and perspectives. It is important to seek to understand as much as it is to be understood. Varying points of view can often have elements of truth to them. But we tend to hold our own opinions in higher esteem than others', and declare them as edicts on the world, when in reality there are just different perspectives.

As we grow in grace, our contentions can be replaced by compassion as we learn to surrender more and more to God's perspectives rather than our own. Putting on the mind of Christ is to seek mercy more than religious rituals and decrees.[52] Mercy grows as we slow down to capture God's perfect peace, right when judgments want to dominate our emotions with rage. I suggest taking a deep breath and searching for the source of our reactions. The Psalmists use the Hebrew concept of *Selah,* which means to take a reflective pause. Practicing *selah* gives our heart the space it needs for mercy and grace to take root and displace the anger we naturally gravitate toward.

A firefighter friend recently shared one of the reasons why he started looking for a new church. His wife had a difficult pregnancy

---

[52] Hosea 6:6ff

that caused her extensive pain and discomfort, so they intentionally sat in the back row and left early to avoid the jostling of the crowds. To me, it seemed like a noble effort for her to even attempt to attend services at all, so imagine how they felt when the pastor called her out from the pulpit for leaving the service a few minutes early. Not knowing her situation, the pastor decided to use them as examples to rebuke the church for not staying seated until the service had fully ended. When my friend shared this story with me, my heart raced with judgment toward this graceless shepherd. But I was quickly convicted of the many times I have been bothered by those who prematurely slip out of the church where I serve. My own thoughts are proof of the fact that we're quick to judge others for the same sins we engage in.

It is no wonder, then, that Jesus confers a blessing on those who pursue unity over division: "Blessed are the peacemakers, for they shall be called the sons of God."[53] The Prince of Peace Himself modeled for us the ultimate example of being a Peacemaker. In the midst of the most horrific injustices, He had every right to condemn

---

[53] Matthew 5:9 NKJV

His accusers. But instead, He chose forgiveness, praying, "Father, forgive them, for they know not what they do."[54]

As we close our brief stroll behind the veil of ministry together, we can't deny the reality of Post-Traumatic Church Disorder. One researcher found that around one-third (27–33%) of the U.S. faith population has been negatively impacted by toxic religious environments.[55] This fact strengthens our opening premise: that hurt people, hurt people, and that those who were hurt by the church often inflict the same pain on others.

Our healing doesn't stem from the reactions we naturally gravitate toward for our own self-protection. Rather, our healing comes from clinging more desperately to the One who gave birth to the Church. After all, righting wrongs is His responsibility, which is why we call Him our Savior. So, remember that:

---

[54] Luke 23:34 ESV
[55] Slade, D., Smell, A., Wilson, E., and Drumsta, R. (2023). "Percentage of U.S. Adults Suffering from Religious Trauma: A Sociological Study," *Society for Human Resource Management* (SHERM 5/1; 1-28.)

God is good, but people are not.

People are broken and messy.

Jesus isn't broken and messy; Jesus is perfect.

Broken people go to church, and the Church is filled with broken people who are hoping to heal.

The Church, however, isn't broken, and neither is Jesus.

Jesus is always good and perfect, no matter how broken everything else is.

Which is why we all need Jesus - but not a religious version of Him.

We need the *real* Jesus, who's able to heal our pain.

And when the *real* Jesus is embraced, He makes us whole again.

Support and Scriptural Encouragements

"Fret not if our classes forget what we say, but pray them to remember what the Lord says."[56]

It is the author's hope that if some of the principles in this little book are forgotten over time, you will continue to remember the truths of God's Word. Below are Scriptures that you might find helpful in your meditations should you go through a tough season of personal challenge.[57] Also, if Dr. Stonier can ever be of support to you or your loved ones, be sure to reach out to him. He can be reached at MickeyStonier@gmail.com or on his cell phone: 619-843-3100.

"You will show me the path of life; in Your presence is fullness of joy; at Your right hand are pleasures forevermore." (Psalm 16:11) *The author's life verse.*

"And this is eternal life, that they may know You, the only true God, and Jesus Christ whom You have sent." (John 17:3) "That I may know Him and the power of His resurrection, and the fellowship of His sufferings, being conformed to His death." (Philippians 3:10) *Make it your continual aim to know Jesus more deeply and intimately.*

Jesus, "who, when He was reviled, did not revile in return; when He suffered, He did not threaten, but committed Himself to Him who judges righteously." (1 Peter 2:23) *Be continually reminded that you serve an Audience of One. Entrust yourself to Him as you abandon yourself to God.*

---

[56] Spurgeon, C.H. *Come Ye Children.*
[57] Scriptures are cited in the *New King James Version Bible* unless otherwise noted.

"So My heavenly Father also will do to you if each of you, from his heart, does not forgive his brother his trespasses." (Matthew 18:35) *Forgiveness is an essential priority to all human relationships. In times of need, consider reading Matthew 6:8-13; 18:21-35.*

"A new commandment I give to you, that you love one another; as I have loved you, that you also love one another. By this all will know that you are My disciples, if you have love for one another." (John 13:35-34) "Beloved, let us love one another, for love is of God; and everyone who loves is born of God and knows God. He who does not love does not know God, for God is love." (1 John 4:7-8) *Let love be your goal in every situation.*

"Pursue peace with all people, and holiness, without which no one will see the Lord: looking carefully lest anyone fall short of the grace of God; lest any root of bitterness springing up cause trouble, and by this many become defiled." (Hebrews 12:14-15) *As you pursue peace in all relationships, bitterness will be confronted at its root.*

"But the fruit of the Spirit is love, joy, peace, longsuffering, kindness, goodness, faithfulness, gentleness, self-control. Against such there is no law." (Galatians 5:22-23) *The fruit of the Holy Spirit is a gauge to evaluate how you are responding in any of life's circumstances.*

"You will keep him in perfect peace, whose mind is stayed on You, because he trusts in You." (Isaiah 26:3) *As you keep your eyes on Jesus, He will keep you in His peace.*

"And about the ninth hour Jesus cried out with a loud voice, saying, 'Eli, Eli, lama sabachthani?' that is, 'My God, My God, why have You forsaken Me?'" (Matthew 27:46) *Jesus also felt "church hurt" and understands injustice. It is Okay to ask "Why?"*

"I am the vine, you *are* the branches. He who abides in Me, and I in him, bears much fruit; for without Me you can do nothing." (John 15:5) *As you abide in a continual relationship with Jesus in prayer and His Word, you will bear fruit. Stay connected to Him as your Source of life.*

"But we all, with unveiled face, beholding as in a mirror the glory of the Lord, are being transformed into the same image from glory to glory, just as by the Spirit of the Lord." (2 Corinthians 3:18; also, Philippians 3:21 and Romans 8:29) *Have grace for yourself and others as you continue to become more and more like Jesus in your process of spiritual growth.*

"Therefore, as the elect of God, holy and beloved, put on tender mercies, kindness, humility, meekness, longsuffering; bearing with one another, and forgiving one another, if anyone has a complaint against another; even as Christ forgave you, so you also must do. But above all these things put on love, which is the bond of perfection. And let the peace of God rule in your hearts, to which also you were called in one body; and be thankful. Let the word of Christ dwell in you richly in all wisdom, teaching and admonishing one another in psalms and hymns and spiritual songs, singing with grace in your hearts to the Lord. And whatever you do in word or deed, do all in the name of the Lord Jesus, giving thanks to God the Father through Him." (Colossians 3:12-17) *Need I say more? In dealing with church hurt, Paul the Apostle had a prescription that has brought healing through the ages—love and forgiveness that will bring peace.*

One final encouragement: In the future, when friendly fire comes your way, duck!

Reflection Questions

The purpose and themes in the booklet, *Post-Traumatic Church Disorder,* are not intended to pull up our painful past to stir up criticism, complaints, judgments, and/or embitterment. But in contrast, it is the intention of this brief study to spend time in personal reflection to bring healing to our church hurts and brokenness. As such, when considering these questions guard your heart from drifting back to old triggers, and direct attention to align with elements of grace, faith, hope, and love. To be sure, injustice is wrong. God's heart is broken over your painful experiences and He is not OK with how you were treated. The Lord knows your pain more than you know. Yet in light of our wounds our focus is to seek for God's healing touch of spiritual courage and forgiveness.

Preface

1.) Truly the church has a lot of brokenness as shown through people demonstrating failure and the sins of the flesh. In contrast, who are the people in your life who display Christ-like character, service, and goodness that are worthy of emulating? Share a few stories together of individuals who represent to you the fruit of the Spirit.
2.) Love and trust are essential to healthy human development from birth. What was your homelife like as you were growing up through childhood?
3.) Due to any family deprivations growing up, have you had any personal struggles with bouts of anger, shame, over-control, and/or chaos? If you can be vulnerable, what are some of these challenges?
4.) Have you demonstrated any "pseudo-self" characteristics to compensate for some of the wounds of your childhood and/or adolescence?
5.) What has encouraged the greatest growth through your journey of church hurt?

Chapter One: *Ministry Behind the Veil*

1.) What are the elements that you love most about the church as God intended the church to be?
2.) How has God used you to bring encouragement, support, growth, and guidance to others in your church involvement?
3.) What are some of the resources that you are aware of where wounded souls could be supported by counsel and/or spiritual healing?
4.) What are some of your gifts, strengths, and temperament style that blesses your community of friends and acquaintances?
5.) What is one thing you seek in church leadership that you could be to others?

Chapter Two: *Two Deadly Questions*
1.) Has there been a time where you were judgmental of another person or situation wherein you were not correct in your evaluation? Share your experience.
2.) Have there been times when you were wrongly judged by others? Without being critical of the offenders, how did you work through that experience?
3.) Are there any areas of pride or insecurity in your life that cause you to be overly self-focused?
4.) Who in your life has helped you get back on track when you've been knocked off course? How did they help you?

Chapter Three: *With-ness Empowers Witness*

1.) Besides the word "with," what are some of the words that you would use to summarize the entire Bible? Why those words?
2.) How has God demonstrated His closeness to you?
3.) What habits and commitments tend to keep you overly busy?
4.) What are the spiritual disciplines through God's grace that you can commit more to that will empower you further in communion with Jesus? (E.g. prayer, fasting, solitude, silence, etc.)

Chapter Four: *Embitterment Disorder*

1.) What has assisted you in overcoming the temptations of bitterness against any injustice done against you?
2.) Who in your sphere of influence do you more need to actively encourage, provide guidance to, invest in, and/or disciple?
3.) In reflection of 1 Peter 1:18-25, are there any encouragements that the Lord speaks to you about following more acutely in the steps of Jesus in the midst of being hurt?
4.) What are things you can do to provide better support to your church leaders to inspire them to greater integrity, humility, and faithfulness?

Chapter Five: *Freedom in Forgiveness*
1.) As you read through chapter five, were you able to walk through the model of forgiveness towards others? If so, what was your experience?
2.) How can you demonstrate more vulnerability and authenticity to those with whom you are in close relationship?
3.) At the end of your life, what would you hope would be your legacy? In other words, what virtues would you desire to display that people would testify about you as to how you lived your life?
4.) What Bible character do you most identify with that relates to your life? Why this individual?

Final Thoughts

1.) As an individual or group, how can you be used to bring more unity in your spheres of influence?
2.) When you feel a surge of potential criticism of a person or situation, what could you do to avoid the spreading of cynical poison to others?
3.) In your recent journey of faith what are some areas where you see that God is giving you victory and/or growth?
4.) In reflection of your reading through *Post-Traumatic Church Disorder*, what are a couple of the greatest takeaways for you to commit to for your future?
5.) Who in your relationship network would benefit through reading this booklet? Consider passing it along to them.

Spend some time praying as an individual or group to grow in intimacy with Jesus as you surrender more to His heart and plans for your life.

Notes

Notes

Notes

Notes

Printed in Great Britain
by Amazon